The Almond Flour Cookbook: 30 Delicious Gluten Free Recipes

by Rashelle Johnson

Disclaimer:

The information contained in this book is for general information purposes only. This book is sold with the understanding the author and/or publisher is not giving medical advice, nor should the information contained in this book replace medical advice, nor is it intended to diagnose or treat any disease, illness or other medical condition.

While we endeavor to keep the information up to date and correct, we make no representations or warranties of any kind, express or implied, about the completeness, accuracy, reliability, suitability or availability with respect to the book or the information, products, services, or related graphics contained book for any purpose. Any reliance you place on such information is therefore strictly at your own risk.

Dedication:

This book is dedicated to my loving husband, who has been there for me through thick and thin and to my children, who have had to endure recipe after recipe in my quest to perfect the almond flour recipes in this book.

Contents

What is Almond Flour?.. 8

Almonds Are Good for You.. 10

How to Use Almond Flour.. 13

Almond Flour and Your Diet...................................... 16

How to Make Homemade Almond Flour 18

Blanching Almonds.. 20

Measuring Almond Flour.. 21

Storing Almond Flour 22

Recipes.. 24

Cherry Berry Almond Smoothie (Gluten-Free) 25

Raspberry Peach Almond Smoothie (Gluten-Free).. 26

Chocolate Peanut Butter Protein Smoothie (Gluten-Free) 27

Almond Flour Pancakes (Gluten-Free) 28

Almond Flour Waffles (Gluten-Free)....................... 30

Gluten-Free Blueberry Cobbler............................... 32

Banana Bread (Gluten-Free).................................... 34

Cranberry-Raisin Granola Bars (Gluten-Free) 36

Gluten-Free Quinoa Raisin Bars 38

Gluten-Free No Grain Blondies 40

Chocolate Chip Cookies (Gluten-Free) 42

Chocolate Chunk Brownie Cookies (Gluten-Free) .. 44

Easy Peanut Butter (and Jelly) Almond Flour Cookies (Gluten-Free) 46

Snickerdoodles (Gluten-Free) 48

Gluten-Free Sugar Cookies 50

Microwave Chocolate Mug Cake (Gluten-Free) 52

Coconut Cupcakes (Gluten-Free) 53

Blueberry Almond Flour Muffins (Gluten-Free) 55

Almond Cinnamon Rolls (Gluten-Free) 57

Almond Flour Toasted Coconut Donuts (Gluten-Free) 59

Chocolate Almond Brownies (Gluten-Free) 61

Cheesy Cheddar Crackers (Gluten-Free) 63

Almond Flour Pie Crust (Gluten-Free and Sugar-Free) 65

Almond Flour Cheese Sticks (Gluten-Free) 66

Almond Flour Crab Cakes (Gluten-Free) 68

Almond Flour Baked Onion Rings (Gluten-Free).... 70

Almond Flour Chicken Tenders (Gluten-Free) 72

Pizza Muffins (Gluten-Free) 74

Almond Flour "Tortilla" Chips (Gluten-Free and Sugar-Free) 76

Hamburger Buns 78

The End 80

What is Almond Flour?

To put it simply, almond flour is a gluten-free flour made by grinding blanched almonds, which are almonds that have had the skin peeled or ground off. Leaving the skin on when almonds are ground gives you almond meal. Almond flour is finer than almond meal in texture and works well as a flour replacement in many recipes.

Almond flour is coarser than the white processed flour you're used to, but it makes for a passable replacement in many recipes that call for processed flour. While there aren't any health benefits to be gained from consuming white flour, almond flour is loaded with nutrients and good fats your body needs to stay healthy.

If you're gluten-intolerant and your body is unable to properly process foods made from grain, almond flour will probably allow you to add many of your favorite foods like breads, cakes and cookies back into your diet. You may not have to give up your favorite foods—you just have to change what they're made of.

Many foods made using almond flour instead of wheat flour taste the same or even better than their counterparts. You probably won't notice much of a difference in taste in most recipes.

Almond flour is low in carbs and sugar, and is high in protein and a number of other nutrients.

A cup of ground almonds contains 20 grams of carbs, 12 of which are fiber. This gives you a net carb count of 8 grams of carbohydrates per cup. Contrast that with 90 grams of carbohydrates in a cup of wheat flour and you begin to see why almond flour is the healthier choice.

Since it consists of only ground almonds, it's a good choice for those on low-carb, gluten-free, Paleo, raw food or clean eating diets. While there are other flour alternatives on the market, you'd be hard-pressed to find one as versatile as almond flour.

Almonds Are Good for You

Here are just some of the health benefits of eating almonds:

- **Good source of vitamin E.** This vitamin is essential if you want healthy skin and hair. It has antioxidant properties and is able to protect your body from damage from free radicals.
- **Good source of copper.** The copper in almonds helps promote healthy bones.
- **Good source of protein.** Almond flour is a great source of protein. A single cup of almond flour contains 20 grams of protein.
- **Eating almonds promotes brain health.** Many of the nutrients found in almonds are good for your brain. Tryptophan is just one of the nutrients in almonds that are good for your brain.
- **Controls bad cholesterol.** Almonds reduce the levels of LDL cholesterol in your body, which is the bad type, while raising the levels of HDL cholesterol, which is the good type.
- **Promotes heart health.** The nutrients in almonds are good for your heart and can help ward off heart disease. The magnesium found in almonds reduces the risk of heart attacks, while the folic acid may help prevent the clogging of arteries.

- **May lower blood pressure.** The potassium found in almonds can help keep high blood pressure in check.
- **Weight loss.** The fats found in almonds are good fats that help regulate appetite and prevent you from overindulging at the dinner table. Consumption of foods containing almond flour may actually help you lose weight, as opposed to foods made from processed flour, which largely cause you to gain weight.
- **Wards off diabetes.** Almonds help regulate insulin levels in the blood, which in turn helps prevent diabetes.
- **Prevention of birth defects.** The folic acid in almonds helps prevent birth defects.
- **High in fiber.** The high levels of fiber in almonds prevent constipation and helps food move through your digestive system.
- **Good for skin, nails and hair.** Almonds have vitamin B, which promotes healthy skin, hair and nails.

While all of these benefits are good, the biggest benefit of almond flour for many is that it allows those who can't handle gluten to continue enjoying items that are made with flour.

It's estimated that a couple million Americans are afflicted with celiac disease, a disorder that makes them intolerant to gluten. It causes digestive problems, prevents the body from absorbing nutrients from food and can cause a number of other issues. At times, this disorder works silently or presents itself in ways that aren't easily associated with consumption of gluten.

If you're having health problems and can't figure out the cause, try cutting gluten out of your diet. Even those who don't test positive for celiac disease may be putting stress on their bodies by consuming gluten. Gluten intolerance is more common than people think, and it's rarely diagnosed, especially in the early stages when symptoms aren't bad or are barely noticeable.

At the very least, processed flour has no health value whatsoever. At its worst, it could be slowly destroying your digestive system and negatively impacting your health. Try making the switch to gluten-free almond flour. Your body will thank you for it.

How to Use Almond Flour

The recipes in this book have been hand-picked and designed to use almond flour. They're a great start for someone looking to learn the ropes cooking with almond flour, but eventually you're going to want to branch out and try new recipes.

The good news is you can use almond flour to replace wheat flour in a large number of recipes. If you have a favorite recipe that calls for flour, try replacing the flour with almond flour. You might find it works just as well, or better, and you'll have a new recipe that's better for you than your old one.

Switching from wheat flour to almond flour isn't always as simple as making a 1:1 swap between the two. Almond flour isn't as dry and fluffy as regular flour, so it can weigh down a recipe and make the resulting product thicker in texture. A cup of almond flour weighs almost a full ounce heavier than a cup of white flour. When you swap almond flour for wheat flour in your recipes, the resulting batter or dough will almost always be thicker. This isn't necessarily a bad thing; it's just something you need to be aware of so you don't overcorrect for it.

The main recipes where almond flour doesn't work as well as regular flour are recipes that require you to knead your flour into dough that combines with yeast to rise. The gluten found in dough is what causes it to thicken up and become elastic when you knead it, so it's tough to make certain types of dough with flour that doesn't have gluten.

Some recipes work better if you add extra egg when you make the switch to almond flour. An extra egg or two can add more structure to the dough. This works in some recipes to get the dough to the correct consistency, but adding too much egg can make your food sticky and gummy. You can try adding a bit of whey protein and extra baking soda.

Foods that you cook using almond flour are going to brown faster than those with wheat flour. To make up for the faster browning, you can either lower the temperature at which you cook the food by up to 50 degrees F or you can reduce the cooking time. You can also cover the pans with aluminum foil and remove for the last 10 minutes or so of baking to give your foods time to brown.

Almond flour works well for the following types of food:

- **Brownies.**
- **Cakes.**
- **Cookies.**
- **Crackers.**
- **Donuts.**
- **Gravies.**
- **Muffins.**
- **Pancakes.**
- **Panini.**
- **Pastries.**
- **Pizza dough.**
- **Quick-rise breads.**
- **Smoothies.**
- **Soups.**

If you aren't sure whether almond flour will work, try it and see. The worst that can happen if you'll have to toss out a batch of dough or something you baked that didn't turn out right. If it works, you'll have a new recipe to add to your bag of tricks, and a healthy recipe, to boot.

Almond Flour and Your Diet

Almond flour is compatible with most diet plans, but there are some things you need to take into consideration. Here are some of the diet plans almond flour works well with, along with the considerations that have to be made:

Clean eating. While whole grain flour is allowed in the clean eating diet, you can replace it with almond flour for even greater health benefits. The almond flour sold in stores is technically "processed," so you're much better off buying locally-grown almonds and making your own almond flour.

Gluten-free diet. Almond flour is gluten-free, so it's a good alternative to wheat flour in a gluten-free diet plan.

Low-carb diet. A low-carb diet requires that you keep carbohydrate consumption to a minimum. Almond flour is a good choice for a low-carb diet because it has less than a third of the carbs of regular flour.

Paleo diet. The Paleo diet plan requires that you eat only foods that our hunter-gatherer ancestors would have had access to. While almond flour is considered a natural food, some Paleo dieticians would recommend against using it because it goes against the ultimate goal of going back to eating to survive instead of eating just because we want to.

Raw food diet. The raw food diet requires that you only eat foods in their natural state. No processing or adding of chemicals is allowed. Raw almonds in the United States are pasteurized or treated to prevent them from going bad, which means they are no longer considered "raw." You may be able to get truly raw almonds from small local orchards. If you can get them, you can make your own almond flour that conforms to the tenets of the raw food diet.

Most diets allow almond flour in at least some of the stages of the diet—and for good reason. It's a healthy alternative to flour that's lower in carbs and is packed full of nutrients. I know some of the low-carb diets like Atkins only allow almond flour in certain stages, so if you're in doubt, ask.

How to Make Homemade Almond Flour

The best way to make almond meal is to purchase blanched almonds from a small local grower and to make the meal yourself. It's cheaper to make your own almond meal and you can make sure there are no chemicals or additional processing involved.

Here are the steps required to make almond flour from blanched almonds:

1. Purchase blanched almonds.
2. Freeze them for 30 minutes. This will allow you chop your almonds up into a finer powder without turning them into paste.
3. Put them in a food processor or blender.
4. Pulse for 5 - 10 second increments and check. Repeat until the almonds are the size of small crumbs. Grinding the almonds for too long will cause them to release too much oil and turn to butter.
5. Once they're the size of small crumbs, set food processor or blender to high and grind for 10 seconds.
6. Sift through a flour sifter and place larger pieces of almond back into the food processor or blender. Continue steps 5 and 6 until all of the almonds have been reduced to flour.

You probably aren't going to get great results if you're using a cheap blender. The cutting blades have to be sharp in order to chop almonds into flour. If they're dull, you'll get pulverized almonds that are more like a paste than a powder.

If you're planning on using your almond flour for items like muffins, doughnuts or waffles, you can stop grinding once the almonds are the texture of corn meal. This will work fine in recipes that don't require powdery flour. There's a fine line between almond flour and almond butter. If you grind your almonds too much, they'll turn into butter. It's still good for you, but not ideal for baking purposes.

Blanching Almonds

If you're feeling industrious, you can buy regular almonds and blanch them yourself. It isn't hard, but will require a bit of work because you have to manually remove the skin from each almond.

Here are the steps required to blanch almonds:

1. Fill a pot with water and bring it to a boil.
2. Remove pot from flame and pour almonds into it.
3. Let them sit in the water until the water cools enough that it's safe to touch.
4. Remove the almonds one at a time and squeeze them between your fingers. They should pop right out of the skin.
5. Set the oven on low and cook the almonds for 15 minutes to dry them out.

Blanch your own fresh almonds straight from the farm and you know you're getting good quality almonds that haven't been processed in any way. I've found that almonds I blanch myself and then dry are the easiest almonds to grind to a fine powder.

Measuring Almond Flour

I get asked all the time whether almond flour should be measured by packing the flour into the cup or by scooping the flour out and leveling it. The answer is . . . it depends. Some bakers prefer to scoop and level their cups, while others pack them tight.

All of the recipes in this book are written using the standard scoop and level technique of measuring out flour. To use this method, you scoop out an overflowing scoop of flour and use a flat instrument like the blade of a knife to level it off. Don't pack the almond flour down.

When I'm searching for new recipes, I often come across recipes that don't indicate which method to use. I always assume it's the scoop and level method and go from there. Most recipe writers know they need to indicate on the recipe when packing the cup is required. You will come across the odd recipe that doesn't indicate this, so if your food doesn't turn out the way you expected it to, you can try recreating the recipe using the packing technique of measuring.

Storing Almond Flour

Almond flour is easy to store.

If you're going to use it in a month or less, place it in an airtight container and store it in your pantry or in another cool, dark place. Almond flour will last up to a month in your pantry as long as you store it in the proper container. Any longer than that and the fats in the flour will start to go rancid. If you store your almond flour on the counter it'll start going bad much sooner. If you open your bag and it smells like it has gone bad, it's probably because the fats have started to turn.

Almond flour lasts a lot longer when refrigerated or frozen.

If you have a lot of almond flour or you have a little, but don't use it very often, place it in a zip-lock baggie and remove as much air from the baggie as you can. Once you've got as much of the air out as possible, you can store your almond flour in the fridge or the freezer. Almond flour will last six months or more in the fridge as long as the container is sealed, but will start to pick up scents and tastes from foods in the fridge after a short while if the container isn't properly sealed. Frozen almond flour lasts for years in the freezer.

Label your containers so you know when you placed them in the pantry, fridge or freezer. That way there's no confusion later on down the road. While you might remember today the exact date you put your almond flour in the freezer, your memory isn't going to be as clear a year down the road.

Make sure you properly store your almond flour and you'll always have tasty, healthy flour to use in your foods. Store it improperly and you'll have an inedible mess.

Recipes

Finally, the section you bought the book for! The following recipes are all tried and true almond flour recipes that are favorites in my kitchen, and in kitchens the world over.

I hope you enjoy these recipes as much as I have!

The almond flour used in these recipes is blanched almond flour. You may be able to substitute almond meal for some of the recipes, but I haven't tried it.

And before you fill my inbox with questions—yes, the recipes in this book are gluten-free. Just make sure you use gluten-free chocolates, which can sometimes have gluten in them because of their ingredients or the manufacturing process.

Cherry Berry Almond Smoothie (Gluten-Free)

I love smoothies. I also love almond flour. It's only natural I found a way to combine the two into a delicious smoothies that's good for you and is filling enough to serve as a meal replacement for those times when you're in a hurry and don't have time to whip up a full meal.

You can add protein powder to this smoothie if you're looking to give it an extra boost. If you add protein powder and are concerned about keeping the recipe gluten-free, double check the powder doesn't contain gluten.

Ingredients:

½ cup almond flour
½ cup almond milk
10 cherries, pitted
10 blueberries
10 blackberries
¼ teaspoon almond extract
2 teaspoons honey
5 ice cubes

Directions:

1. Add all ingredients to a blender and blend until smooth.
2. Serve immediately.

Raspberry Peach Almond Smoothie (Gluten-Free)

Here's another one of my favorite smoothie recipes. This raspberry peach smoothie is a great meal replacement.

Add protein powder to it if you want to up your protein intake. Again, if you add protein powder and are concerned about keeping the recipe gluten-free, double check the powder doesn't contain gluten.

Ingredients:

¼ cup almond flour
¼ cup almond milk
1 cup peaches, sliced
1 cup raspberries
3 tablespoons honey
5 ice cubes

Directions:

1. Add all ingredients to a blender and blend until smooth.
2. Serve immediately.

Chocolate Peanut Butter Protein Smoothie (Gluten-Free)

This shake is for the bodybuilders amongst us. It's packed clear full of protein, what with the peanut butter and the protein powder. To keep this smoothie gluten-free, make sure your protein powder doesn't contain gluten. Some protein powders have ingredients added that contain gluten. You're also going to want to double check the peanut butter to make sure it doesn't have any gluten.

Ingredients:

1 cup unsweetened almond milk
¼ cup almond flour
½ cup chocolate protein powder
4 tablespoons peanut butter
5 ice cubes

Directions:

1. Blend ingredients together and serve immediately.

Almond Flour Pancakes (Gluten-Free)

Breakfast is one of my favorite meals of the day. When I decided to give up gluten, I thought I was going to have to give up my favorite breakfast meal, a big stack of pancakes covered with fruit. And I did at first, until I realized almond flour works every bit as well as wheat flour to make pancakes. Now, I can enjoy my favorite breakfast whenever I want.

This recipe makes 8 medium-sized pancakes. If the batter is too thick for your tastes, try adding more water to thin it out. If you want it thicker, add more almond flour.

These pancakes can be cooked up and served hot, or you can whip up an entire batch of them and put them in the freezer. When you want to reheat them, pop them in the toaster and toast until warm.

Ingredients:

¾ cup almond flour
2 large eggs
1/8 cup water
1 tablespoon vanilla extract
1 tablespoon honey
¼ teaspoon baking soda
¼ teaspoon salt
Almond oil, for cooking

Directions:

1. Add ingredients together and whisk until smooth.
2. Add more water if you want thinner batter.

3. Add oil to skillet and heat skillet of medium heat.
4. Scoop 3 to 4 tablespoons of batter onto skillet for small pancakes or 5 to 6 tablespoons for larger pancakes.
5. Let cook on first side until brown.
6. Flip and brown the other side.
7. Stack finished pancakes on a plate and add your favorite topping.
8. Serve hot.

Almond Flour Waffles (Gluten-Free)

These almond flour waffles taste great and are a good replacement for the wheat flour waffles you're probably used to eating. I swapped them out without saying anything to my kids and they didn't notice the difference. This recipe is gluten-free.

This recipe will make 5 to 6 waffles.

Ingredients:

1 cup almond flour
2 eggs
½ cup milk
2 tablespoons brown sugar
1 teaspoon vanilla
1 ½ teaspoons cinnamon
½ teaspoon baking soda
¼ teaspoon salt

Directions:

1. Add all of the ingredients to a mixing bowl and mix until incorporated.
2. Heat up your waffle iron while the mixture sits out in the open air.
3. Follow the instructions that came with your waffle iron as to how much batter to use and how long to cook your waffles. Remember that waffles with almond butter will cook faster than regular waffles, so you need to keep a close eye on them.
4. Remove finished waffle from iron.

5. Serve warm.

Gluten-Free Blueberry Cobbler

Got extra blueberries laying around that you aren't sure what to do with? Neither do I, but this recipe is good enough that you should pick some up next time you're at the store. If you can't get fresh blueberries, the frozen ones work almost as well. You can also use other fruits like strawberries, raspberries or blackberries. You may have to adjust the amount of maple syrup you add as sweetener.

I like to make blueberry cobbler for breakfast on those cold mornings when you want something warm that sticks to your ribs. My kids will eat it any time of day.

Topping Ingredients:

1 ½ cups almond flour
¼ cup butter
1 teaspoon cinnamon
Almond slices, to taste
2 tablespoons maple syrup

Filling Ingredients:

2 cups blueberries
½ cup lemon juice
4 tablespoons maple syrup
3 tablespoons arrowroot starch
¼ teaspoon sea salt

Directions:

1.   Preheat oven to 350 degrees F.

2. Add all of the filling ingredients to a mixing bowl and stir until combined.
3. Place the filling in a baking dish and spread it out evenly.
4. In a separate bowl, combine the almond flour, butter, cinnamon and almond slices. Mix until crumbly.
5. Sprinkle the topping over the filling.
6. Drizzle maple syrup over the topping.
7. Bake for 20 to 25 minutes, or until the filling starts to bubble.
8. Let cool for 10 minutes and serve while warm.

Banana Bread (Gluten-Free)

This bread is low-carb, free of added sugar and gluten-free. It's also absolutely delicious. It works well with breakfast and is great for snacks or dessert. No matter what time of day it is, you'll find yourself looking for reasons to eat a piece—and you can do it guilt-free.

Ingredients:

3 cups almond flour
1 cup ripe bananas, mashed
1 teaspoon Stevia
2 egg whites
½ cup water
2 teaspoons vanilla
1 tablespoon Xanthan gum
¾ teaspoon salt
1 teaspoon baking powder

Directions:

1. Add dry ingredients to a mixing bowl and stir until mixed.
2. Add wet ingredients to a second bowl and blend until smooth.
3. Mix wet and dry ingredients and stir until incorporated.
4. Preheat oven to 350 degrees F.
5. Divide dough into two 3 X 6 bread pans.
6. Bake for 30 to 40 minutes, or until a toothpick inserted in the middle comes out clean.

7. Cool and serve.

Cranberry-Raisin Granola Bars (Gluten-Free)

This recipe is gluten-free as long as the oats you use aren't contaminated with gluten. Since oats are often processed in facilities alongside other grains, they can sometimes get cross-contaminated. Gluten-free steel cut oats are available, so they may be a good option if you're looking to completely eliminate gluten from your diet.

Ingredients:

1 cup almond flour
1 cup gluten-free steel cut oats
½ cup almond slices
½ cup dried cranberries
½ cup raisins
1 tablespoon sesame seeds
1 tablespoon chia seeds
½ teaspoon salt
¼ cup honey
3 ½ tablespoons coconut oil
½ teaspoon vanilla extract
¼ teaspoon almond extract
¼ cup pecan halves

Directions:

1. Add honey, coconut oil, vanilla extract and almond extract to a saucepan and heat until it starts to bubble.
2. Combine the dry ingredients in a mixing bowl.

3. Pour the wet mixture into the dry mixture and stir until all of the dry ingredients are coated.
4. Place parchment paper in the bottom of a 9 X 13 baking dish.
5. Spread the mixture evenly in the dish.
6. Cover the dish with plastic wrap and place in the fridge for 6 hours.
7. Remove from dish and cut into bars.
8. Store uneaten bars in the fridge until you decide to eat them.

Gluten-Free Quinoa Raisin Bars

This is one of my all-time favorite almond flour recipes. When I add chocolate chips to the recipe instead of raisings, my kids go wild for it, too. They'll eat it with raisins, but there's a bit of whimpering about how much better the bars are when they have chocolate chips.

Ingredients:

1 cup almond flour
½ cup yellow corn flour
½ cup potato starch
¾ cup quinoa flakes
2 cups brown sugar
½ cup coconut oil
2 large eggs
1 cup raisins
2 tablespoons maple syrup
2 tablespoons vanilla extract
2 teaspoons cinnamon
1 teaspoon xanthan gum
1 teaspoon sea salt
1 teaspoon baking powder
1 teaspoon baking soda

Directions:

1. Preheat oven to 350 degrees F.
2. Whisk dry ingredients together in a large mixing bowl.

3. Stir in the wet ingredients until you get a smooth dough.
4. The dough should be moist and sticky. If it's too dry add a few teaspoons of milk at a time and stir the milk in until the dough feels right.
5. Line a 9 X 11 baking pan with parchment paper and spread the dough evenly in the pan.
6. Bake for 25 to 30 minutes, or until the bars start to brown around the edges.
7. Remove from oven and place on a wire rack to cool.
8. Cut into squares and serve. Refrigerate the bars you don't eat. If you won't be eating them for a while, you can also freeze these bars.

Gluten-Free No Grain Blondies

There's no doubt about it; blondies are delicious. There's also no doubt that regular blondies are packed full of processed sugar and white flour and aren't good for you. These blondies completely eliminate processed sugar and grain from the equation and are a much better choice when you want something sweet.

Ingredients:

1 ½ cups almond flour
¼ cup butter, melted
½ cup honey
1 large egg
½ cup unsweetened coconut
½ cup gluten-free semi-sweet chocolate chips
½ cup walnuts
¼ teaspoon baking soda
¼ teaspoon salt
1 tablespoon vanilla extract

Directions:

1. Preheat oven to 350 degrees F.
2. Melt butter in saucepan over low heat. Stir in honey and vanilla.
3. Add almond flour, egg, baking soda and salt to a large bowl and stir until incorporated.
4. Pour melted butter mixture into the bowl and stir until incorporated.
5. Add the rest of the ingredients and stir in.

6. Line an 8 X 8 baking pan with parchment paper and spread the batter evenly into the pan.
7. Sprinkle chocolate chips on top if you want.
8. Bake for 15 minutes, or until a toothpick entered into the middle comes out clean.
9. Let cool, slice into squares and serve.

Chocolate Chip Cookies (Gluten-Free)

This quick and easy chocolate chip cookie recipe is gluten-free and good for those trying to steer clear of wheat flour. Make sure the chocolate chips you use are made in a gluten-free facility or you may run the risk of getting contaminated chips.

Ingredients:

1 ½ cups almond flour
¼ cup coconut oil, melted
¼ cup clover honey
1egg
1 cup chocolate chips
½ tablespoon vanilla extract
¼ teaspoon salt
½ teaspoon baking soda

Directions:

1. Combine all ingredients in a large bowl and mix until incorporated.
2. Preheat oven to 350 degrees F.
3. Remove 1 ½ tablespoons of batter and place it on a parchment paper-lined cookie sheet. Leave a couple inches space between each cookie.
4. Bake for up to 15 minutes, checking frequently after 10. The cookies are done once they've begun to brown.
5. Remove from oven and let cool on the cookie sheet for 5 minutes.

6. Transfer to a wire rack and let finish cooling.

Chocolate Chunk Brownie Cookies (Gluten-Free)

These cookies are rich, moist and full of chocolate. They're absolutely delicious, too, and won't last long once you remove them from the oven. These are the cookies my kids ask me to make when they have friends over and my husband asks for these whenever he has a potluck at work.

If you want this recipe to truly be gluten-free, make sure the chocolate you use is gluten-free.

Ingredients:

1 ½ cups almond flour
½ cup melted bittersweet chocolate
½ cup bittersweet chocolate, chopped into chunks
½ cup unsweetened cocoa
2 eggs
1 stick butter
1 cup coconut sugar
¾ teaspoon sea salt
¾ teaspoon baking soda
1 ½ teaspoons vanilla extract

Directions:

1. Combine the almond flour, coconut sugar, baking soda, salt and cocoa in a mixing bowl.
2. Add the melted chocolate, butter, eggs and vanilla and beat until smooth.
3. Fold the chocolate chunks into the dough.
4. Preheat your oven to 350 degrees F.

5. Place tablespoons of dough 3 inches apart on a parchment-lined baking sheet.
6. Bake for 10 minutes. Cookies should be soft to the touch when you remove them from the oven.
7. Let cool on baking sheet for 5 minutes and transfer to a wire rack to finish cooling.

Easy Peanut Butter (and Jelly) Almond Flour Cookies (Gluten-Free)

This recipe can be made with or without the jelly. Without the jelly, you get peanut butter cookies that are packed with protein and other nutrients. With it, it's like having a PB & J sandwich in cookie form. Either way, you get tasty cookies that are much better for you than regular peanut butter cookies.

This recipe is gluten-free as long as the jam you use doesn't have gluten. Most jams are gluten-free, but there is the occasional oddball jam that uses flour as a thickener.

Ingredients:

1 ½ cups almond flour
1 egg
½ cup natural peanut butter
¼ cup coconut oil
½ cup coconut sugar
¼ teaspoon sea salt
¼ cup of your favorite jelly

Directions:

1. Place wet ingredients (except for jelly) in a mixing bowl and blend until creamy.
2. Stir in remaining ingredients.
3. Scoop out teaspoons of dough and roll them into balls.
4. Preheat oven to 350 degrees F.

5. Place on cookie sheet and press down on the center of the dough ball with your thumb to make a well into which you can place jelly.
6. Fill the well you created in each cookie with jelly.
7. Bake for 10 to 12 minutes, or until done.
8. Let cool on cookie sheet for 5 minutes. Transfer to wire cooling rack to finish cooling.

Snickerdoodles (Gluten-Free)

Snickerdoodles are one of my favorite cookies. They've been a guilty pleasure of mine for years, and I'm sure they're responsible for a number of the extra pounds I've had to lose via working out and healthy eating. This recipe allows me to enjoy all of the goodness of snickerdoodles without experiencing the guilt.

They're gluten-free, too, as are the rest of the recipes in this book. You can enjoy these cookies without worrying about what the gluten in them is doing to your body.

This recipe makes approximately 1 dozen cookies.

Cookie Ingredients:

1 ½ cups almond flour
½ cup brown sugar
¼ cup butter
2 tablespoons shortening (can substitute palm shortening or coconut oil to make healthier)
4 tablespoons honey
1 teaspoon vanilla
1 large egg
½ teaspoon baking soda
½ teaspoon salt
1 teaspoon cinnamon

Topping Ingredients:

½ cup sugar (you can use sugar substitutes if you like, but snickerdoodles taste best with regular sugar)
2 teaspoons cinnamon

Directions:

1. Let butter sit out until it begins to soften.
2. Blend honey, brown sugar, butter and shortening until smooth.
3. Add eggs, vanilla, salt, cinnamon and baking soda and blend until smooth.
4. Add almond flour slowly while blending. When you're done the dough should be able to be rolled into balls. If it's too runny, try adding more almond flour.
5. In a small bowl, mix the topping ingredients until incorporated.
6. Roll the cookie dough into balls and roll the balls around in the sugar-cinnamon topping until they're coated in sugar.
7. Preheat oven to 350 degrees F.
8. Line a baking sheet with parchment paper and place dough balls on the sheet. Leave a couple inches space between each ball.
9. Cook for 10 to 12 minutes. Check after 10 to see if done.
10. Let cool for 5 minutes on the baking sheet, then transfer over to a wire rack.

Gluten-Free Sugar Cookies

If you're anything like me, when the holidays roll around, you start craving sugar cookies. This recipe uses almond flour instead of white flour to create dough that can be cut into whatever shape you want. Decorate them and let your kids dig in, knowing they're eating cookies made from flour that's good for them.

Ingredients:

2 cups almond flour
¼ cup clover honey
2 tablespoons coconut oil, melted
3 tablespoons applesauce
1 tablespoon vanilla extract
¼ tablespoon baking soda
A pinch of sea salt

Directions:

1. Combine dry ingredients and stir until incorporated.
2. Combine wet ingredients in a separate bowl and stir until blended.
3. Combine the dry and wet ingredients and mix thoroughly.
4. Wrap the resulting dough ball in plastic wrap and place it in the fridge for 45 minutes. This step is important because it will firm the dough up.
5. Lightly dust a piece of parchment paper with almond flour and set the dough down on it.

6. Dust another piece of parchment paper and place it over the top of the dough.
7. Roll the dough out until it's ¼-inch thick.
8. Preheat oven to 350 degrees F.
9. Use your cookie cutters to cut out the shapes you want your cookies to be. If the dough gets too warm and becomes soft, return it to the fridge for a while to firm up.
10. Place cookies on a parchment-lined cookie sheet and bake for 8 to 12 minutes. They're done when they start to turn brown around the edges.
11. Let the cookies cool on the cookie sheet.
12. Decorate and serve.

Microwave Chocolate Mug Cake (Gluten-Free)

This recipe is designed to be made in a coffee mug. It's a single-serving chocolate cake. You can make it sugar free by substituting the sugar for Splenda. I've tried it both ways and prefer it with sugar, but if you're trying to cut back on your sugar intake, it's still pretty good with Splenda.

Ingredients:

¼ cup almond flour
1 egg
3 tablespoons sugar
3 tablespoons butter, melted
2 tablespoons cocoa powder
1 tablespoon water

Directions:

1. Add ingredients to a large microwavable coffee mug.
2. Stir them with a fork until blended.
3. Microwave on high for 1 to 1 ½ minutes.
4. Let cool and served topped with whipped cream.

Coconut Cupcakes (Gluten-Free)

These cupcakes are dense and moist and downright delicious. Best of all, your friends and family won't know you're feeding them something that's good for them unless you want them to. I'll leave it up to you whether you want to tell them or not.

This recipe makes 8 cupcakes.

Ingredients:

½ cup almond flour
1 cup desiccated coconut
½ cup shredded coconut
1 ½ teaspoons coconut flour
2 tablespoon coconut oil
1/3 cup coconut milk
3 eggs
½ cup honey
1 teaspoon vanilla extract
1 teaspoon baking powder
1/3 teaspoon salt

Directions:

1. Mix desiccated coconut, shredded coconut, coconut flour, baking powder and salt in a large bowl.
2. In a separate bowl, mix the rest of the ingredients together.
3. Combine the contents of the two bowls and mix until incorporated. You don't want to blend the batter too much. It should be combined, but not smooth.

4. Preheat oven to 350 degrees F.
5. Place cupcake liners into a muffin tin.
6. Fill cupcake liners with batter until they're ¾-full.
7. Bake for 20 to 25 minutes. Check by inserting toothpick into the middle. If it comes out clean, the cupcakes are done.
8. Place cupcakes on wire rack and let sit until cool.

Frosting Ingredients:

1 cup coconut oil, melted
2 cups powdered sugar
1 cup shredded coconut
½ cup coconut creamer
1 teaspoon vanilla extract

Frosting Directions:

1. Add ingredients except ½ cup of shredded coconut to mixing bowl and beat on medium until blended.
2. Bump your blender up to high and beat until fluffy.
3. Wait until cupcakes are cool to top them with this frosting.
4. After topping cupcakes, sprinkle shredded coconut on top.

Blueberry Almond Flour Muffins (Gluten-Free)

These blueberry muffins are all but indistinguishable from regular blueberry muffins. They have a slightly nutty aftertaste, but that adds to the flavor rather than detracting from it. If you're craving a blueberry muffin, this is a good gluten-free choice.

This recipe makes 6 muffins. Double it to fill a tin that holds 12 muffins.

Ingredients:

1 cup almond flour
½ cup blueberries
1 egg and 1 egg white
½ teaspoon baking soda
½ teaspoon cinnamon
1 tablespoon coconut oil
1 teaspoon vanilla extract
2 tablespoons honey
½ tablespoon apple cider vinegar

Directions:

1. Mix all ingredients except blueberries together in a large bowl.
2. Blend until smooth.
3. Fold blueberries into batter.
4. Preheat oven to 350 degrees F.
5. Place cupcake liners in muffin tin and fill liners almost to the top.

6. Bake for 20 to 25 minutes or until a toothpick comes out clean.
7. Place muffins on a cooling rack and let cool.

NOTE: If these muffins aren't sweet enough for your tastes, try sprinkling a bit of raw sugar on top.

Almond Cinnamon Rolls (Gluten-Free)

These cinnamon rolls are a great choice for those mornings when you wake up and want a comfort food. I remember waking up to warm, gooey cinnamon rolls as a kid and to this day, smelling cinnamon rolls baking brings me back to my childhood and makes me happy. The frosting contains quite a bit of sugar, so I don't recommend eating these all the time, but they make for a great treat every once in a while.

Cinnamon Roll Ingredients:

2 ½ cups almond flour
¼ cup coconut oil, melted
2 large eggs
2 tablespoons clover honey
½ teaspoon salt
½ teaspoon baking soda
¼ teaspoon vanilla extract
¼ teaspoon ground cinnamon

Filling Ingredients:

½ cup clover honey
½ cup toasted almond slices
¼ teaspoon ground cinnamon
¼ cup raisins (optional)

Frosting Ingredients:

½ cup coconut butter, melted

3 teaspoons agave nectar

Directions:

1. Preheat oven to 350 degrees F.
2. Combine dry ingredients in a mixing bowl.
3. Combine wet ingredients in a separate bowl. The eggs need to be room temperature for best results.
4. Combine the wet and dry ingredients and knead into dough.
5. Let sit in fridge for 15 minutes to thicken it up.
6. Roll out a piece of parchment paper and sprinkle almond flour on it.
7. Roll out the dough.
8. Time to add the filling! Drizzle honey over the dough and sprinkle almond slices, cinnamon and raisins liberally across the surface.
9. Roll the dough into a log. You have to be gentle or it will break apart.
10. Cut the roll into slices.
11. Line a baking tray with parchment paper and place cut rolls on the tray.
12. Cook for 12 to 15 minutes. Watch the rolls closely and remove them when the start to brown.
13. Remove from oven and let cool for 5 minutes.
14. Mix coconut butter and agave nectar.
15. Drizzle frosting over the top and serve warm.

Almond Flour Toasted Coconut Donuts (Gluten-Free)

I'm almost embarrassed to admit it now, but a few years ago I was addicted to donuts. I absolutely had to have a tasty Dunkin' Donut at least 2 mornings a week when I was on my way to work. It didn't help that I worked less than a mile from a Dunkin' Donut shop.

I'd be lying to you if I told you these donuts were as good as Dunkin' Donuts or Krispy Kremes, but they are pretty good. They're also much better for you and won't pack on the pounds like the regular donuts do. I still crave Dunkin' Donuts from time to time, but I'm able to fight off those cravings with this recipe.

You can switch toppings out to whatever you'd like. Cinnamon and sugar works well, as does chocolate frosting.

Ingredients:

1 ½ cups almond flour
5 eggs
3 tablespoons clover honey
1 ½ teaspoons vanilla extract
¼ teaspoon salt
½ teaspoon baking soda

Topping Ingredients:

4 tablespoons honey
¼ cup toasted coconut

Directions:

1. Add all of the ingredients to a large bowl and whisk together until incorporated.
2. Fill donut maker (or donut circles) with batter and shut the lid on the donut maker.
3. Cook for 3 to 5 minutes or until donuts start to brown.
4. Let cool.
5. Drizzle honey on top of each donut and sprinkle toasted coconut liberally on top.

Chocolate Almond Brownies (Gluten-Free)

I had a tough time getting this brownie recipe right. I originally had more almond flour in it and the brownies came out too crumbly. Then I added more egg and they came out way too thick. I adjusted the recipe for a third time and I think these are just right.

They're moist, but not too moist, and they're rich enough that you don't have to frost them—unless you want to. If you do decide to frost them, go with something light, like a drizzling of caramel or maple syrup.

Ingredients:

1 cup almond flour
½ cup butter
2 cups unsweetened chocolate, chopped into small pieces
¼ cup semi-sweet chocolate chunks
1 cup cane sugar
2 eggs
1 teaspoon vanilla extract
½ teaspoon baking powder

Directions:

1. Preheat oven to 350 degrees F.
2. Add butter and unsweetened chocolate to a saucepan over medium heat. Stir until chocolate melts and combines with butter.
3. Add the sugar, eggs and vanilla to the saucepan and stir it in.

4. Add the almond flour, cane sugar and baking soda to a mixing bowl and stir until combined.
5. Pour wet ingredients into the mixing bowl with the dry ingredients and stir until incorporated.
6. Spread batter evenly into a baking dish.
7. Press chocolate chunks into the top of the batter.
8. Bake for 25 to 30 minutes, or until the edges start to brown and pull away from the sides of the pan.
9. Leave in pan and let cool for at least 15 minutes before serving.

Cheesy Cheddar Crackers (Gluten-Free)

One of my sons loves Goldfish crackers. While he isn't gluten-intolerant, I'm always looking for healthier alternatives to the foods I feed my kids, so I decided to try to make something gluten-free and healthy.

I tried this recipe with just almond flour and it didn't turn out very well, so I added in the gluten-free flour mix. Try it both ways to see which you prefer. You may like the recipe with just the almond flour.

Ingredients:

¾ cup almond flour
¾ cup gluten-free flour mix
½ cup cheddar cheese, grated
¼ cup unsalted butter, softened
¼ teaspoon garlic powder
¼ teaspoon paprika
½ tablespoon sea salt
3 tablespoons water

Directions:

1. Add all ingredients except water to a mixing bowl and blend on low speed until incorporated.
2. Add water a tablespoon at a time and blend until the dough starts to ball up and stick to your blender blades.
3. Sprinkle almond flour on a flat surface and knead the dough into a ball.
4. Wrap in plastic and chill for 45 minutes.

5. Preheat oven to 375 degrees F.
6. Lightly coat two sheets of parchment paper with almond flour and roll out the dough between the sheets. The dough will be dry and is going to want to crack and split, so you're going to have to work it slowly.
7. Cut the rolled dough into the shapes you want your crackers to be.
8. Line a baking sheet with parchment paper and place crackers on the paper.
9. Bake for 8 to 10 minutes, or until crackers start to brown around the edges.
10. Let dry on baking sheet and store in an airtight container until serving.

Almond Flour Pie Crust (Gluten-Free and Sugar-Free)

This is an easy-to-make pie crust that works well for most applications. Fill it with whatever you like. From pumpkin pies to banana crème pies, this pie crust gets the job done. This crust is gluten- and sugar-free. The pie filling you use will ultimately determine whether the finished product is the same.

Ingredients:

2 cups almond flour
¼ cup unsalted butter
¼ teaspoon salt
1 egg white

Directions:

1. Mix all of the ingredients together until incorporated.
2. Spread out in a greased pie pan.
3. All you have to do is add the filling and bake your pie.

Almond Flour Cheese Sticks (Gluten-Free)

These cheese sticks are a great alternative to the pre-made highly-processed cheese sticks sold in the frozen foods section at your local grocery store. Once you try these, you're never going to want to eat the processed ones again.

Ingredients:

1 cup almond flour
3 large eggs
1 tablespoon Italian seasoning
1 ½ cups coconut oil
10 to 12 sticks of Mozzarella cheese

Directions:

1. Place cheese sticks in freezer at least an hour before preparation. You can buy Mozzarella string cheese, or you can cut your own sticks from a block of fresh cheese. I prefer to cut my own because the string cheese sticks undergo more processing and don't taste as good.
2. Place eggs in small dish and beat.
3. Mix almond flour and Italian seasoning in a separate bowl.
4. Add coconut oil to saucepan and heat it on medium heat.
5. Dip each cheese stick into the egg and roll them around.

6. Dip them into the almond flour mixture and roll them around until coated.
7. Place each cheese stick into the saucepan and fry until golden brown. This will only take a couple minutes.
8. Place finished cheese sticks on a towel-lined plate and let sit for 5 minutes.
9. Serve warm with ranch dressing or marinara sauce.

Almond Flour Crab Cakes (Gluten-Free)

When I set out to find the perfect almond flour crab cake recipe, what I wanted was something that was a passable substitution for my recipe that called for wheat flour. What I got was something that ended up being so much better than my original recipe that I was shocked. These crab cakes have a firm, crunchy outside with just a hint of almond flavor and a soft, chewy inside, which is exactly what you want in a crab cake.

This recipe makes 6 medium-sized crab cakes.

Ingredients:

1 ½ cups almond flour
½ pound crab meat, shredded
¼ cup gluten-free mayonnaise
¼ cup corn meal
1 egg
2 tablespoons Dijon mustard
½ tablespoon cilantro
¼ tablespoon garlic powder
½ tablespoon dill, chopped
½ teaspoon sea salt
A pinch of pepper
2 teaspoons lemon juice
½ cup olive oil

Directions:

1. Whisk wet ingredients together in a mixing bowl.

2. Add 1 cup of almond flour and the herbs and stir until combined.
3. Add crab and fold it into the mix. Try to keep large clumps of crab from breaking up.
4. Divide crab mixture into 6 patties of equal size.
5. Chill for 45 minutes.
6. Mix remaining almond flour and corn meal in a small bowl.
7. Coat patties with almond flour/corn meal mixture.
8. Add olive oil to skillet and heat it up over medium heat.
9. Place crab cakes in the oil and cook until browned on both side.
10. Remove crab cakes from oil and place on a paper towel-lined plate to drain.
11. Let cool for 5 minutes and serve warm.

Almond Flour Baked Onion Rings (Gluten-Free)

This is a healthy alternative to deep fried onion rings. I guess you could deep-fry these if you want to, but they're tasty enough baked that I haven't even considered it. They're a great side when you want something the kids will eat.

This recipe will make enough batter for 24 onion rings.

Ingredients:

1 cup almond flour
2 onions, sliced into rings
2 large eggs
2 tablespoons half-n-half
½ teaspoon almond powder
½ teaspoon paprika
½ teaspoon garlic powder
A pinch of salt
A pinch of black pepper
Olive oil

Directions:

1. Add eggs, half-n-half and salt and pepper to a mixing bowl and whisk together.
2. Place onion rings in the batter and let sit while you create the breading.
3. Add the rest of the ingredients(except the olive oil) to another bowl and stir until incorporated.

4. Remove onion from the batter and place it in the breading. Flip it over a couple times to ensure the entire onion ring is coated with breading.
5. Preheat oven to 375 degrees F.
6. Place coated onion rings on a baking sheet lined with foil. Brush the foil with olive oil before setting the onion rings on it.
7. Bake for 8 to 10 minutes, flip and bake another 8 to 10 minutes, or until golden brown.
8. Remove from oven. You can sprinkle the onion rings with salt before serving if you want, or you can serve them as-is with some sort of dip.

Almond Flour Chicken Tenders (Gluten-Free)

Chicken nuggets are a favorite lunch item for my kids. The problem with the nuggets you buy from the store is they're so processed that the meat inside hardly resembles chicken anymore. I got sick of it and decided to come up with something healthier. These chicken tenders use chicken breasts and almond flour to create a healthier nugget made from real chicken.

Serve your kids these instead of the highly-processed nuggets they're used to and they'll be begging for more. You can whip up a big batch ahead of time and freeze them. When lunch time rolls around, all you'll have to do is grab them out of the freezer and pop them in the oven.

Ingredients:

1 cup almond flour
1 pound boneless skinless chicken breasts
2 eggs
1 teaspoon garlic powder
½ teaspoon oregano
¼ teaspoon paprika
½ teaspoon pepper
½ teaspoon salt

Directions:

1. Preheat oven to 375 degrees F.
2. Shred chicken and hammer it with a meat tenderizer.
3. Add all ingredients (except chicken and eggs) to a mixing bowl and stir until incorporated.

4. Place eggs in a small bowl and whisk.
5. Take a chunk of chicken and roll it into a ball.
6. Dip it in the egg and then roll it around in the topping.
7. Place finished tenders on a baking tray and bake for 8 to 12 minutes or until the outside turns golden brown.
8. Let cool for 5 minutes and serve warm with ranch dressing or barbecue sauce to dip them in.

Pizza Muffins (Gluten-Free)

I grew up in a small town in the middle of nowhere that didn't have a pizza place nearby. When we went into town, it was always a treat if we got to go to the local pizza joint. Maybe that's why I love these pizza muffins so much . . . Or maybe it's because they're absolutely delicious. My husband grew up in a larger town and had pizza regularly and he loves these muffins, too.

This recipe makes 12 muffins. As long as you make sure the ingredients you use are gluten-free, this recipe is gluten free.

Ingredients:

1 cup almond flour
½ cup butter, melted
2 large eggs
½ cup pepperoni, cut into small cubes
¾ cup Mozzarella, shredded
¼ cup Parmesan, grated
1 teaspoon baking powder
¼ teaspoon garlic powder
¼ teaspoon oregano
A pinch of salt

Directions:

1. Preheat oven to 350 degrees F.
2. Whisk dry ingredients until incorporated.
3. Stir in the wet ingredients and cheeses. Save ¼ cup of Mozzarella cheese and ¼ cup of pepperoni pieces.

4. Place 12 cupcake liners in a muffin tin and fill each liner evenly with batter.
5. Bake for 15 minutes. Sprinkle remaining pepperoni and Mozzarella on top of each muffin.
6. Bake for another 5 to 10 minutes, or until the cheese browns and starts to bubble.
7. Remove from oven and let cool for 10 minutes on a wire rack.
8. Serve while warm.

Almond Flour "Tortilla" Chips (Gluten-Free and Sugar-Free)

These tortilla chip clones work well in homemade nachos and are great with guacamole and salsa. The key to making these "chips" work is rolling them out as flat as possible. It's going to take some work on your part to get them flat enough, but the reward is a tasty and crunchy chip that works well for most applications in which you'd use tortilla chips.

Ingredients:

3 cups almond flour
3 egg whites
¼ teaspoon onion powder
¼ teaspoon garlic powder
¼ teaspoon cumin
¼ teaspoon cayenne pepper
¼ teaspoon ground coriander
2 teaspoons sea salt
¼ cup water

Directions:

1. Preheat oven to 350 degrees F.
2. Mix almond flour, egg whites, onion powder, garlic powder, cumin, cayenne pepper, ground coriander and 1 teaspoon of sea salt together until it forms into dough.
3. Dust a piece of parchment paper with almond flour.
4. Set the dough on the parchment paper.

5. Dust a second piece of parchment paper with almond flour and set it on top of the dough.
6. Roll the dough out as flat as you can get it.
7. Remove the top layer of parchment paper.
8. Cut the dough into strips or triangles.
9. Bake for 5 minutes.
10. NOTE: Steps 10 and 11 are optional. Combine ¼ cup water with sea salt and stir until salt has dissolved.
11. Lightly brush the chips with the saline solution.
12. Bake for 3 to 5 more minutes. The chips will be lightly browned when they're done. Keep a close eye on them because some chips will finish before others.
13. Remove the chips and let them cool.

Hamburger Buns

Yes, you can be on a gluten-free diet and still enjoy a tasty burger every once in a while! I've got to warn you that these buns aren't exactly like the hamburger buns you're used to, but they're passable and will allow you to make gluten-free burgers and breakfast sandwiches. It took me a couple sandwiches to get used to them, but now I think I like them better than regular buns.

You're going to need a muffin top pan to make these buns. If you try to make them without the right pan, you're going to get dry, crumbly edges on your buns that break apart when you handle them. They're still edible, but tend to be a bit messy.

Ingredients:

1 cup almond flour
1/3 cup unsalted butter, melted
3 medium eggs
2 teaspoons baking powder
A pinch of salt

Directions:

1. Preheat oven to 350 degrees F.
2. Add dry ingredients to a large bowl and stir together.
3. Add wet ingredients and whisk together until incorporated.
4. Lightly grease muffin top pan with butter.
5. Divide batter into 6 equal portions and place in muffin top pan.

6. Bake for 15 minutes or until done. The buns will be done when they begin to brown around the edges.
7. Remove from oven and place buns on a wire rack to cool.

The End

Thanks for purchasing this book. I hope you enjoy the recipes in this book as much as I have. If you have any comments or questions, drop me a line at:

mike_rashelle@yahoo.com

If you enjoyed the book, please take the time to check out my other cookbook:

The Quinoa Cookbook: Healthy and Delicious Quinoa Recipes (Superfood Cookbooks)

http://www.amazon.com/The-Quinoa-Cookbook-Delicious-ebook/dp/B00B2T2420/

CPSIA information can be obtained at www.ICGtesting.com
Printed in the USA
LVOW12s1925280414

383561LV00027B/955/P